ENGLISH 1
MATTERS

CLARE CONSTANT · SUSAN DUBERLEY

Heinemann

Contents

*Spelling resource sheets will be found on pages 50 – 79
of the Teacher's File.*

Throughout this book you will find the following cross-references:

TRF The Teacher's File provides support for the activity.
PAGES 00–00

SKILLS The Skills Book offers skills practice related to the activity.
PAGES 00–00

SEE ALSO Other pages in the book will help you with the activity.
PAGES 00–00

The activities in this book have been colour coded:

• specific speaking and listening: pink

• reading: yellow

• writing: blue

• specific language work: beige.

3

Switch on!

1.1

Work in pairs. Ask each other the questions below. Be ready to tell the class what you found out.

1 Which is your favourite television programme, and why?

2 Which evening has the best programmes?

3 Who is your favourite person on television, and why?

4 What is the saddest thing you have ever watched?

5 Which advertisement do you like best?

1.2

Read this passage. Rick and Rose are brother and sister.

Rick and his mates all watched horror videos. Rose had watched some too. Well, she hadn't exactly watched. She had her hands over her eyes for most of the time. She had begged Rick to fast forward the really nasty parts. But Rick had said they were the best bits.

Then Mum had caught them. They were both curled up on the sofa. They were watching a monster movie.

A head had just exploded in slow motion.

Mum had exploded in very fast motion.

She had thrown the video in the rubbish bin. Then she had acted like she wanted to throw Rick in the rubbish bin too.

Adapted from *Video Rose* by Jacqueline Wilson

1.3

Work on your own. Answer the questions below.

1 Who often watched horror videos?

2 What did Rose do when the horror video was on?

3 What did Rose ask Rick to do to the video?

4 Where were Rose and Rick when Mum came in?

5 What did Mum do when she saw the video?

1.4

Write about how people in the story feel about horror videos. Copy out and finish these sentences.

1 Rose thinks horror videos are …

2 Rick thinks horror videos are …

3 Mum thinks horror videos are …

1.5

What do you think about horror videos? Copy out and complete this sentence.

I think that horror videos are … because …

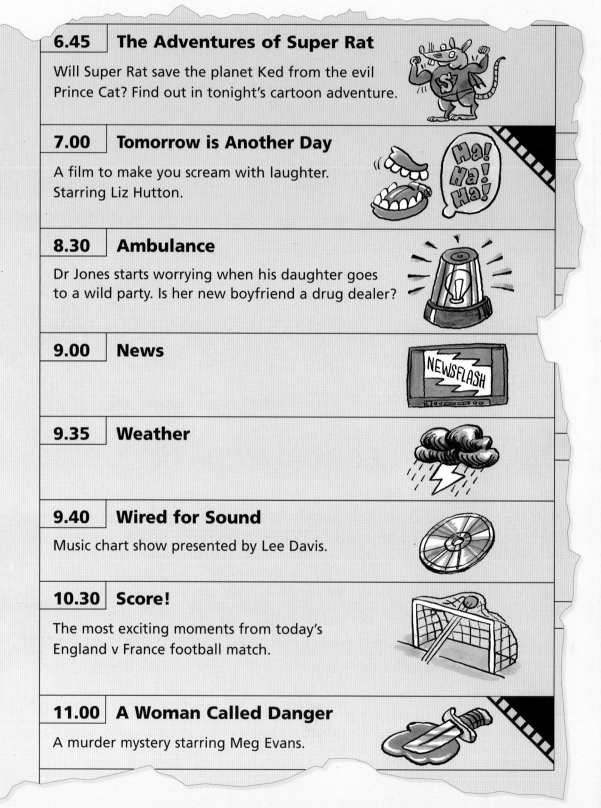

6.45 | **The Adventures of Super Rat**

Will Super Rat save the planet Ked from the evil Prince Cat? Find out in tonight's cartoon adventure.

7.00 | **Tomorrow is Another Day**

A film to make you scream with laughter. Starring Liz Hutton.

8.30 | **Ambulance**

Dr Jones starts worrying when his daughter goes to a wild party. Is her new boyfriend a drug dealer?

9.00 | **News**

9.35 | **Weather**

9.40 | **Wired for Sound**

Music chart show presented by Lee Davis.

10.30 | **Score!**

The most exciting moments from today's England v France football match.

11.00 | **A Woman Called Danger**

A murder mystery starring Meg Evans.

1.7
SKILLS
PAGE 6

Which programme opposite do you think each person below would watch?

1 **Dave** is 15 and loves to keep up with all the latest chart music.

   Dave enjoys Wired for Sound.

2 **Anna** loves anything to do with sport.

3 **Nassim** is six and has to be in bed by 8.00pm.

4 **Sarah** is a big fan of Liz Hutton.

5 **Sarah's mum** wants to watch a murder mystery.

1.8
TRF
PAGE 12

SKILLS
PAGE 7

You are going to plan an evening's television viewing.

1 Match each programme with the time you think it should start. Use a chart like the one below. Children's programmes should be shown earlier.

   Film: Cold Murder   EastEnders   News

   The Bill   Tom and Jerry   Film: Lion King

Time	Programme	What it is about
6.20	Tom and Jerry	More cartoon fun with the crazy cat and mouse pair
6.30		
8.00		
8.30		
9.00		
9.30		

2 Now add a sentence saying what you think each programme is about.

Read this poem. Then answer the questions opposite.

Jimmy Jet and his TV Set

I'll tell you the story of Jimmy Jet –
And you know what I tell you is true.
He loved to watch his TV set
Almost as much as you.

5   He watched all day, he watched all night
Till he grew pale and **lean**,
From *The Early Show* to *The Late Late Show*
And all the shows between.

He watched till his eyes were frozen wide,
10 And his bottom grew into his chair.
And his chin turned into a **tuning dial**,
And **antennae** grew out of his hair.

And his brains turned into TV tubes,
And his face to a TV screen.
15 And two knobs saying 'VERT' and '**HORIZ**'
Grew where his ears had been.

And he grew a plug that looked like a tail
So we plugged in little Jim.
And now instead of him watching TV
20 We all sit around and watch him.

By Shel Silverstein

---

lean – thin
tuning dial – a knob you turn to change channels
antennae – long thin aerials (you say it *an-tenni*)
VERT and HORIZ – controls for the size of the picture

1.10

Answer these questions about the poem.

1 When does Jimmy watch television?

2 What is the **first** thing that happens to Jimmy because he watches so much television?

3 How does Jimmy's head change?
   Use a chart like this to help you:

His eyes were …
His chin turned into …
Antennae grew …
His brains …
His face …
His ears …

4 How does Jimmy's body change? List **two** ways.

5 Look at the end of the poem. What has Jimmy become?

1.11

Read the poem again. Then look at the picture below.

The artist did not read the poem very carefully before drawing Jimmy.

1 Discuss the mistakes the artist made. Look for **five** things. Make a list of them.

2 Which things did the artist get right?

1.12

Writing in sentences

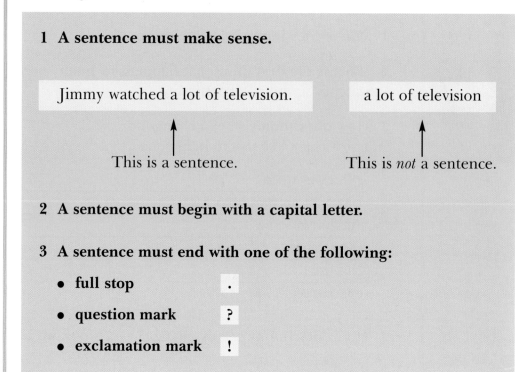

1 **A sentence must make sense.**

| Jimmy watched a lot of television. | a lot of television |

This is a sentence.   This is *not* a sentence.

2 **A sentence must begin with a capital letter.**

3 **A sentence must end with one of the following:**

- **full stop**   .
- **question mark**   ?
- **exclamation mark**   !

1.13

Which of these are sentences? Write out the sentences.

1 I like to watch

2 Jimmy had seen every video in the house.

3 Liz had taken the wrong

4 I lost the

5 Meg looks terrible in that film.

1.14

SKILLS
PAGES 8, 9

Join words in lists A and B together to make sentences. Write out each sentence that you make. For example:

The film has finished now.

A	B
1 The film	**a** the whole match.
2 Gary missed	**b** watch the horror film.
3 I do not want to	**c** **has finished now.**
4 It is time	**d** are my favourites.
5 James Bond films	**e** for the news now.

1.15

TRF
PAGE 13

Re-write the jumbled sentences below so they make sense.

1 is called *Wildlife on One*. The show

2 a lot It teaches about animals. you

3 My was about favourite programme tigers.

4 Tigers feed on cattle deer. and

5 not many tigers the world left in. There are

When Simon watches television he eats a TV snack. Look at what he needs to make it.

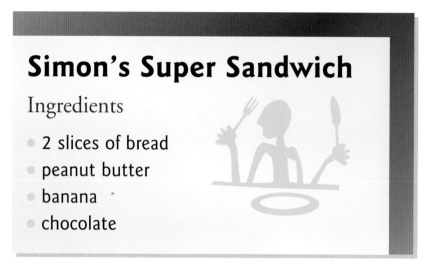

Simon's Super Sandwich

Ingredients

- 2 slices of bread
- peanut butter
- banana
- chocolate

TRF
PAGE 14

SKILLS
PAGE 10

Now look at the pictures on the opposite page.

Write a sentence for each picture explaining how Simon makes his sandwich. The sentences have been started for you.

1 First Simon spreads …

2 Then he slices …

3 He puts the …

4 Next he grates …

5 Then he spoons …

6 After that he …

7 Then Simon cooks it in … for …

8 Finally the sandwich is …

Check that all your sentences:

- make sense
- begin with a capital letter
- end with a full stop.

Simon's Super Sandwich

2 I'm so hungry!

2.1 **Read the story on the opposite page. Mr Hannay is the new school cook. His cooking is rather strange.**

2.2 **Read each sentence below. Decide whether each sentence is true or false. Make a list of your answers.**

1 Mrs Trafford says that Mr Hannay has gone to the gym.

2 Opek is a white mush and it tastes horrible.

3 Sam finds a shoe tag in his dinner.

4 Jane thinks the children have been eating old P. E. kit.

2.3

TRF
PAGE 16

SKILLS
PAGE 11

List six things in your art room that Mr Hannay could use to make lunch. Work out the menu. Answer the questions below to help you.

1 What three things can he put in the main course?

2 What is the main course going to be called?

3 What three things can he put in the pudding?

4 What is the pudding going to be called?

2.4

TRF
PAGE 16

Write out the menu. Make it sound tempting. It should look like the menu in the picture opposite.

A Dish Called Opek

On Wednesday Jane and Sam decided they would
only eat school lunch if they knew what it was.

Sam said, 'How can we find out what it is?'

'We will ask,' Jane told him.

5   At eleven o'clock she put up her hand. She
asked to go to the toilet. But she went to the
kitchen instead. Mr Hannay wasn't there. Mrs
Trafford, the head teacher, was.

'Where's Mr Hannay?' asked Jane.

10   'He's just slipped along to the gym, dear.
Why? Who wants him?' said Mrs Trafford.

'Oh, nobody,' said Jane. 'I was wondering
what was for dinner, that's all.'

'Opek,' said Mrs Trafford.

15   'Pardon?' said Jane.

'Opek. It's a very old dish. Mr Hannay says it's very nice.'

Opek turned out to be a grey mush. It didn't look like
much but it tasted fine.

Everybody was enjoying it.

20   Then Gaz Walker fished out a small, flat object from his
plate. He held it up.

'Here,' he said, 'Why is there a Size 4 tag in my dinner?'

'Let's have a look.' Jane took the tag and **examined** it.
It looked like the sort of tag you'd find inside a shoe.

25   'Opek,' Jane said to herself. She wondered why Mr
Hannay had been in the gym. He should have been in
the kitchen cooking their dinner. 'Opek.' An idea came
into her head. The idea sank slowly into her stomach. It lay
there like a lead weight. She put the tag on the rim of her

30 plate. Then she sat back with her hands across her stomach.
All around the table kids stopped eating. They were
watching her.

'What's up, Jane?' Gaz's voice was husky.

'Opek,' whispered Jane. 'I think I know what it means.'

35   'What does it mean?' asked Sam. He had almost cleared
his plate.

'I think OPEK stands for Old P. E. Kit,' said Jane.

Adapted from *What's for Dinner?* by Robert Swindells

MENU

Don't miss today's tasty treat!

Main Course: OPEK £1

Pudding:
Mixed Sock Pie 60p

Drink:
Shower Juice 20p

SIZE 4

examined – looked at very carefully

2.5

Look carefully at the wrapper below. Then answer the questions.

Front of wrapper

Cadbury's

Caramel

The Big easy...

POCKET PACK

ⓔ 85g

**FIVE GENEROUS FINGERS OF
MILK CHOCOLATE WITH CARAMEL**

Back of wrapper

Ingredients: milk chocolate (milk, sugar, cocoa mass, cocoa butter, vegetable fat, emulsifiers, E442 and E476, flavourings), glucose syrup, hydrogenated vegetable oil, whey syrup, sugar, salt, emulsifier, E471, flavourings.

BEST BEFORE

28 JUL 98

L7283C1

STORE IN A COOL DRY PLACE

9 780863 881848

Milk chocolate: milk solids 14% minimum.

Nutrition Information		Per bar	Per 100g
Energy	kJ	1735	2050
	kcal	410	490
Protein	g	4.0	4.8
Carbohydrate	g	53.0	62.2
Fat	g	20.7	24.6

At Cadbury we are proud of the quality of our products and we want you to enjoy them. If you are not entirely satisfied with this product, please return it with its wrapper to our Consumer Services Manager at the address below, saying when and where it was brought. If bought in the republic of Ireland, please return to Cadbury Ireland Ltd., Coolock, Dublin 5.
CADBURY LIMITED, BOURNVILLE, BIRMINGHAM, B30 2LU UK.

BY APPOINTMENT TO
H.M. THE QUEEN
COCOA AND CHOCOLATE
MANUFACTURERS
CADBURY LTD.
BOURNVILLE

2.6 | **Look at the front of the wrapper.**

   1 What is the chocolate bar called?

   2 Who made the chocolate bar?

   3 Which words in capitals tell you what the bar is made of?

2.7 | **Work in pairs. Look at the whole wrapper.**

   1 Which colours have been used on this wrapper?

   2 List four things that make the wrapper look attractive.

   3 List the types of information you can see on the back.
     ingredients, nutrition details ...

2.8
TRF
PAGE 17

SKILLS
PAGES 12–13

You are going to invent a new chocolate bar.

   1 Write about what is in your chocolate bar. Choose three
     ingredients from the list below. Complete the sentence:
     A chocolate bar made of two fingers of fudge and ...

     chocolate   nuts   toffee   biscuit   cherries

       raisins   caramel   marshmallow

   2 What name will you give your chocolate bar?

   3 Who is it made by? Make up your own company name.

2.9
TRF
PAGE 17

Now draw an eye-catching wrapper for your chocolate bar.

   Use larger letters to write:
   • the name of the bar
   • what is in it
   • who it is made by.

Read this poem carefully. The boy in the poem is thinking about stealing something from a shop. It is as if he can hear a little voice inside him persuading him to do it.

Shoplifting

'I dare you!'
    says a little voice
    soft and sly and very wicked.

'You can show them
5   you ain't chicken
    you ain't **yeller**

  – Are you? Are you?'
  *

'I dare you!'
    says a little voice
10   from deep inside.

'Show them all that
    you're a man
    you're tough and hard

  – You can do it! You can do it!'
  *

15 'I dare you!'
    says the little voice.
    'It's easy, anyone can do it

Show them what you're made of –
    – Quick! Now!
20   Do it! Do it! Do it! Do it!'
  *

           By Mick Gowar

yeller – yellow (afraid)

2.11

TRF

PAGE 18

Work in pairs. Get ready to read the poem aloud.

1 Look at the poem. Which words are said by the 'little voice'?

2 Choose who will read the 'little voice'. The other person reads the rest of the poem.

3 Decide how to say different parts of the poem. Remember the 'little voice' is tempting the boy to steal sweets. Write your ideas in a chart like the one below.

Line	Who is speaking	How to say it
1	The little voice	in a soft, wicked whisper
2–3		

4 Join with another pair. Read the poem to each other.

2.12

Should the boy listen to the voice? Give reasons for your answer.

2.13

Find the three * marked on the poem.

Imagine that a good voice speaks whenever there is a *. It is trying to stop the boy from stealing. Write down what it would say each time. The first speech has been started for you.

No! No! No!
You don't need to prove ...

Nouns

1 A **noun** is a word used to name:

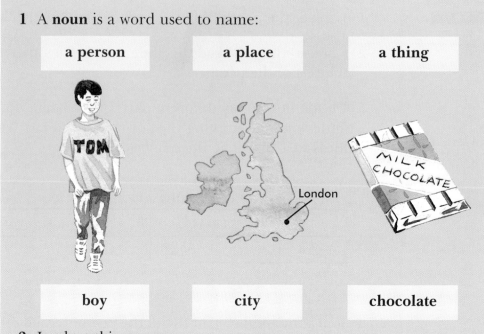

| a person | a place | a thing |

| boy | city | chocolate |

2 Look at this sentence:

When **Tom** went to **London** he took some **chocolate** with him.

All the words printed in **bold** are nouns.

2.15

Look at the picture. List the presents
Tom could have bought in London.
Each word will be a noun.

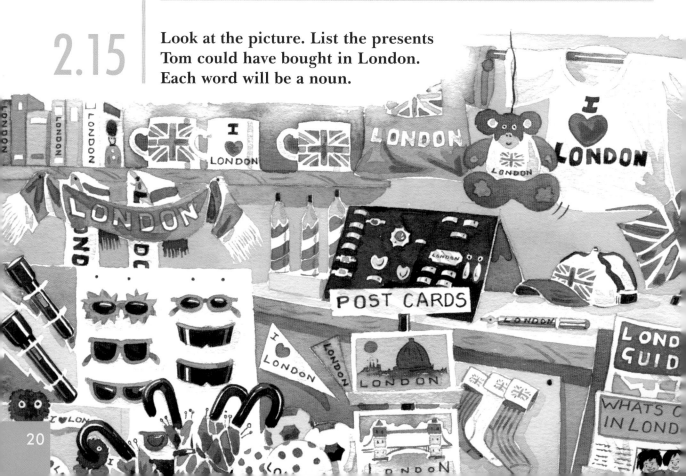

2.16

Write out the sentences below. Put in the missing nouns.

1 When it was time for lunch, Tom went to a _____ .

2 He was going to meet his _____ there.

3 He caught a _____ as it was too far to walk.

4 The _____ asked him where he wanted to go.

5 When he got there he ate a very large _____*cock*_____ .

2.17

SKILLS

PAGE 14

Read the sentences below. List the nouns in each one.

1 London is a very big city.

2 You can travel by bus, train or Tube.

3 It has wonderful cafés and shops.

4 You can buy clothes, CDs and posters.

5 Tom is going to London again when he has enough money.

2.18

Get into groups of four. Play this alphabet game. All your answers will be nouns.

The first person thinks of an object they might see at Pizza Express. It must be one word. It must begin with **a**.

> I went to Pizza Express and I saw some **a**pples.

The second person continues with an object beginning with **b**.

> I went to Pizza Express and I saw some **a**pples and **b**acon.

The third person continues with an object beginning with **c**.

> I went to Pizza Express and I saw some **a**pples, **b**acon and **c**...

- If none of you can think of a word for one of the letters, move on to the next letter.

- Keep taking it in turns until someone forgets the list, or you come to the end of the alphabet.

2.19

Imagine you are going for a meal at Pizza Express. Answer these questions. Give your answers as a list of nouns.

1 What is your favourite pizza topping?

2 What is your favourite drink?

3 What don't you like eating?

4 Which three people would you most like to eat with?

2.20

TRF
PAGE 19

Which pizza topping would each person below choose?
Write your answers in sentences. Underline the nouns.

| tuna | peppers | cheese | tomato | ham | mushrooms |

1 Tom likes fish and meat on his pizza.
  Which two toppings did he choose?

2 Kate is a vegetarian. She does not eat meat or fish.
  Which four toppings did she choose?

3 Tomatoes are the only vegetables that Claire likes.
  Which four toppings did she choose?

2.21

Have you eaten out somewhere? Was it at a friend's house, a café,
on a picnic, or somewhere else?

Write a few sentences about your meal out. Say:

- where you went

- what you ate

- who you were with.

Underline all the nouns in your sentences.

UNIT 3 Strange but true?

3.1 Work in pairs. Read each advertisement. Decide which of the six characters on the opposite page wrote it. When you have finished there will be one picture left.

a

Headless giant (3 metres tall) would like to meet beautiful lady giant (must be over 280 kilos). PO Box 735, Trent.

b

DRAGONS FOR SALE. Make excellent children's pets. Also good if your house is cold in winter. ☎ Phone ☎ Mumblethorpe 6767.

c

Lost: one SKINNY black cat. Answers to the name of **Igor**. Left ear missing, bad-tempered, has a nasty bite. Much missed, **reward offered** for safe return.

Cobweb Cottage, Hobble-on-the Hill.

d

EASY-GOING OGRE needs a home. Good cook, fond of young children. Phone Ugly Town 9967.

e

For sale: ★ ☽ ★ **One broomstick** hardly used. Will swap for lady's bicycle. Phone Skipwick 969.

Adapted from *Small Ads* by Colin West

Look carefully at the picture which did not match an advertisement.

1 Who is it?

2 What does it want? Why?

3 How will people get in touch with it?

Write the advertisement. Look back at the opposite page for help.

3.3

Read the story opposite about Peter's holiday.

Stop reading when you reach a question in a green box.
Decide what is going to happen next in the story.
Then read on, and see if you were right.

3.4

Finish the sentences below. Look at the story to help you.

1 The Martian called when Peter had been on holiday for …

2 Peter answered the …

3 The Martian wanted to …

4 Gran told Peter to look in …

5 The space ship had gone, leaving …

3.5

Work in pairs. Take it in turns to be the Martian answering a question. Help each other work out what to say.

1 How did you feel when your space ship had to land?

2 What were Peter and his Gran like?

3 How did you feel when you could not see your space ship?

4 Why did you go back to Peter's house?

5 How did Peter and his Gran help you to get back home?

3.6

TRF
PAGE 21

SKILLS
PAGES 22–23

Work on your own. Write the Martian's diary.

The Martian will want to write about:
- the space ship having to make an emergency landing
- meeting Peter and Gran
- how it felt when it was left behind
- how it got back home.

Today was going well until our spaceship …
I …

The Visitor

It was on the second day of Peter's holiday. He was staying with his grandmother. There was a knock at the cottage door and Peter went to open it. On the doorstep was a small green **Martian** with webbed feet. It had eyes on the end of short
5   **antennae**. It said very politely:

'I wonder if I might bother you for the loan of a spanner?'

'Sure,' said Peter. 'I'll ask my Gran.' Peter found his Gran and said, 'There's a Martian at the door who'd like to borrow a spanner.'

> What do you think Peter's Gran will say?

10   Gran looked at him over her knitting. 'Is there, dear? Have a look in Grandad's toolbox, there should be one there.' Peter found the spanner and took it back to the Martian.

The Martian held out a rather odd-looking hand and thanked Peter warmly. 'We've some trouble with the gears or
15   something. We had to make an emergency landing. Now the mechanic says he has left his tools behind. Anyway – thanks a lot. I'll bring it back in a minute.'

The Martian padded away up the lane. Peter went back inside. After three minutes there was a knock at the door.

> Who do you think it will be?

20   It was the Martian, looking very upset. It said, 'My space ship has left without me.'

Adapted from A *Martian Comes to Stay* by Penelope Lively

Martian – a person who lives on the planet Mars
antennae – long thin feelers (you say it *an-tenni*)

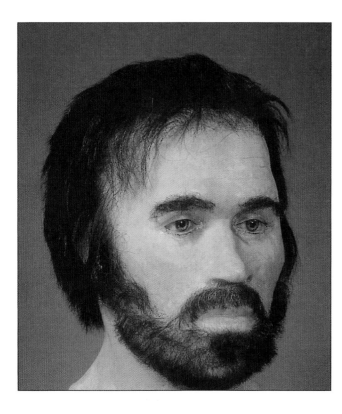

A man's dead body was found in Lindow Marsh in the county of Cheshire. At first police thought they would have to search for his murderer. Then scientists found out that the body was several thousand years old! 5 10

The scientists were able to tell the police a lot about the dead man.

They thought the man looked about twenty-five years old. He had been very strong and fit. 15 He had dark hair and a beard which had been trimmed with scissors. His finger nails had also been cut neatly. Round his arm was a band made of fox fur. 20

They also told the police that he had eaten a burnt crust of bread for his last meal. Then he had been hit over the head and killed.

The police were right. The dead man had been murdered. But they knew they would never find his murderer!

Adapted from *In Search of the Past: Mummies, Masks and Mourners* by Margaret Berrill

3.8 Write the answers to these questions in sentences.

1 How old was the man when he died?
The man was about twenty-five when he died.

2 What was the man's hair like?

3 What was the man wearing on his arm?

4 What had the man eaten for his last meal?

5 How did the man die?

3.9 Imagine you are the policeman who found the body. Write your notes about what happened.

- Today's date is …

- The time is …

- I'm at Lindow …

- Someone has been …

- I think we should …

3.10 The discovery of Lindow Man is going to be on the radio. Write the newsflash telling people about it.

Write at least six sentences. Put in all the information listeners will want to hear. You may like to start like this:

Newsflash!
Today a dead body was dug up at Lindow Marsh in Cheshire. The police said …

Proper nouns

1 A **noun** is a word used to name a thing, person or place:

   county is a noun.

2 A **proper noun** is the name given to one particular person or place. It should begin with a capital letter:

   Cheshire is a proper noun.

   There are many counties but only one called Cheshire.

Cheshire

Places:
- city is a **noun**
- London is a **proper noun**

People:
- man is a **noun**
- John is a **proper noun**

3.12

Try this word game.

The names below are all proper nouns. Re-arrange the letters to spell a noun. The first one has been done for you.

1 Pam

   The letters in the proper noun Pam can spell the noun map.

2 Pat

3 Liam

4 Neil

5 Trish

3.13

Which of these words are proper nouns?

dragon   Snowdon   Clare   sea   shop   Nile

3.14

Write down the answers to these questions. Your answers should be proper nouns.

> 1 Which famous person would you like to meet?
>
> 2 Which town do you live in or nearest to?
>
> 3 What is your favourite name?
>
> 4 Which river flows through London?
>
> 5 Which country would you like to visit?

Check that your answers begin with capital letters because they are proper nouns.

3.15

TRF

PAGES 20, 22

Get into groups to play this proper noun game.

> Your teacher will give you a word which is a noun.
> For each letter of the word you have to think of:
>
> • a proper noun which is the name of a place
> • a proper noun which is the name of a person.
>
> The first game has been started for you:
> The noun is *man*.

Proper nouns			
places	**M**anchester	**A**frica	**N**...
people	**M**ary	**A**ndy	**N**...

Desert Island

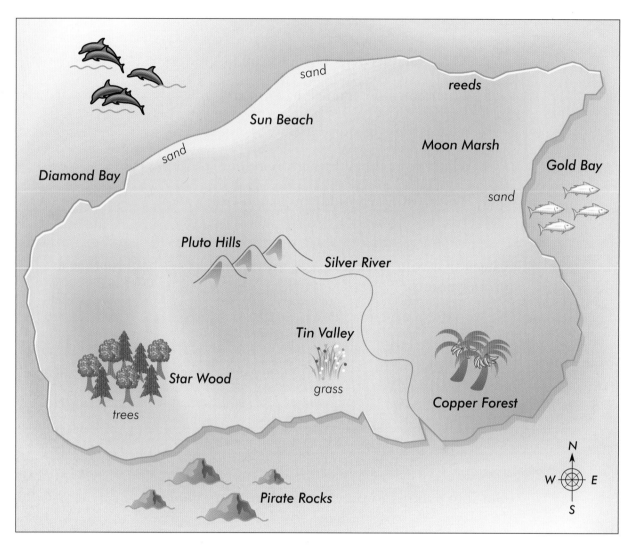

3.16 | **You are going to be left alone on this desert island for a week.**

1 Think of three people you would miss while you are away.

2 Write a few sentences about why you would miss each of them.

> **Person 1: Jack**
> I would miss my best friend Jack most of all. Jack always makes me laugh …
> **Person 2: …**

Look carefully at the map of the island. Find a good place to do each of the following things. Write your answers in sentences:

1 I would collect fresh water at ... because ...

2 I would build a fire near ... because ...

3 I would build my shelter at ... because ...

4 I would go fishing at ... because ...

5 I would pick fruit at ... because ...

Check that you started each name with a capital letter because it is a proper noun.

3.18

Some nouns on the map are not proper nouns. Write down what they are and the place where you will find them:

You will find sand at Diamond Bay and Gold Bay.

Who's bored? Not me!

4.1 **Read the story of Peter Fortune on the opposite page. He is always daydreaming.**

1 Stop when you reach a question in a green box. What might happen next? Read on and see if you were right.

2 What does the story say Peter was inventing?

3 What happened because Peter was daydreaming?

4.2

SKILLS

PAGE 28

Work in pairs. Decide what would happen if Peter was asked to:

1 Take his little sister to school on the bus.

2 Watch the sausages cooking under the grill.

3 Buy some bread for his mother.

4.3 **Work on your own. Plan one of your above ideas as a story. Set it out like this:**

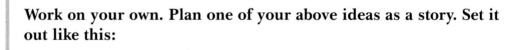

STORY PLAN	
Beginning	Peter is asked to …
Middle	Peter begins to do as he is asked but then he begins to daydream about …
End	because Peter is daydreaming … (say what goes wrong)

4.4

TRF

PAGE 24

Now write your story. Use your plan to help you.

The Daydreamer

One Christmas Peter's father, Thomas Fortune, was hanging the decorations in the living-room. It was a job he hated. It always put him in a bad mood. He had decided to tape some streamers high in one
5 corner. In that corner was an armchair. Sitting in that armchair doing nothing in particular was Peter.

What is Thomas Fortune going to ask Peter to do?

'Don't move, Pete,' said Thomas Fortune. 'I'm going to stand on the back of your chair to reach up here.'
10 'That's fine,' Peter said. 'You go ahead.'
Up on the chair went Thomas Fortune, and away in his thoughts went Peter. He looked like he was doing nothing. In fact he was very busy. He was inventing an exciting way of coming down a
15 mountain quickly. It used a coat hanger and a length of wire. The wire was stretched tightly between the pine trees. Thinking about the mountain air made Peter hungry. He remembered the chocolate biscuits in the kitchen. Meanwhile, Peter's father stood on
20 the back of the armchair. He was straining and gasping as he reached up to the ceiling.

What is Peter going to do?
What will happen to Thomas Fortune?

It was a pity not to eat the biscuits. As Peter stood up, there was a terrible crash behind him. He turned just in time to see his father fall head
25 first into the gap between the chair and the corner.

What will Thomas Fortune do?

Thomas Fortune re-appeared, head first again. He looked ready to chop Peter into tiny bits. On the other side of the room stood Peter's mother. She clamped her hand to her mouth to hide her laughter.
30 'Oh, sorry, Dad,' Peter said. 'I forgot you were there.'

Adapted from *The Daydreamer* by Ian McEwan

Local newspapers often have a 'What's On' page. It tells you about things to do in the area in which you live. Read the 'What's On' page below.

WHAT'S ON?

Circus School

Come and learn how to spin plates, walk on globes and juggle. We will even teach you how to fly through the air on a **trapeze**! Classes are held every Saturday 10.00am–12.30pm.
Cost: £5.00 per session.
Circus School is held at The Big Top School, Eden Road, West Gorton.
Book your place NOW by calling 01986 4440.

Fast Tech

Enjoyable after-school club. We teach children how to use computers. Bring your homework project or try our quizzes and games. Club nights are Monday, Wednesday and Friday.
Held at the Youth Centre, Mill Road, Sonting.
Ring 896948 for details.

Canley Swimming Pool

Have you heard about Canley's exciting new pool? This pool offers *much* more than the chance to swim lengths. Our wave machines, slides and whirlpools are simply the best. If you want to relax there is a great beachside setting. Phone 589324 for details.

The Great Balloon Experience

We're sure you've seen our gold hot air balloon **hovering** above West Witting. But did you know that you can take a mini-flight in it? At only £15 for a thrilling 15 minutes we know you will want to find out more. Call Golden Rides on 497545 for details.

trapeze – a swing used in a circus
hovering – hanging in the air

4.6

The people below have just read the 'What's On' page. Which place should each of them phone?

1 Carla's Grandad will soon be 60. She wants to give him a birthday present he will always remember.

2 Next Friday John wants to take his youth club on a trip. They have just finished exams. They will be full of energy.

3 Suni would love to learn how to juggle. He wants to amaze his friends.

4.7

TRF
PAGE 25

Choose one of the 'What's On' activities and re-read it. Design a poster to advertise it. Use the steps below to help you plan it.

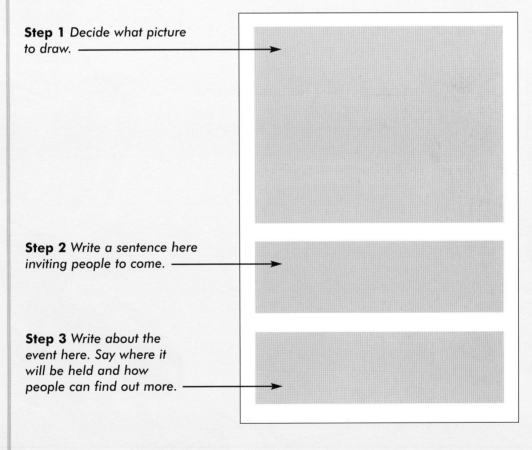

Step 1 *Decide what picture to draw.*

Step 2 *Write a sentence here inviting people to come.*

Step 3 *Write about the event here. Say where it will be held and how people can find out more.*

4.8

Now draw your poster. Important words that you want people to read first should be in a larger size.

Read the poem.

Alone in the House

I like being left alone
When everyone's gone out.
I change from Channel 1 to 3
And from 3 to 4 to 2,
5   I play the music centre
As loud as it will go,
I call up Dial-a-Recipe
And talk back to the voice,
Search the fridge and larder
10   For leftover luxuries,
Put pickled onions and bananas
In my giant sandwiches,
I crunch the solid icy peas
Straight from the freezer tray
15   And write notes to our milkman
'Three hundred pints today.'
I creep round in the darkness
Pretending I'm a burglar or a cat,
I slither head first down the stairs
20   In my brother's sleeping bag
And I read the books my sister
Keeps hidden from my dad.
Then …
I sit down with my sandwich
25   In my father's favourite chair
Put my feet on the table
And feel glad that they're not there
… once in a while.

By Trevor Millum

300 PINTS TODAY

4.10

Read the questions below. Choose the right answer.

1 What does the poet like to do with his music centre?
  a) He likes to play his favourite records.
  b) He likes to play his music really loudly.

2 Why does he like phoning Dial-a-Recipe?
  a) He can hear a voice reading out recipes.
  b) He can talk to the voice.

3 What does his note tell the milkman?
  a) His note tells the milkman that they need lots of milk.
  b) His note tells the milkman not to leave any milk today.

4 Who does he pretend to be?
  a) He pretends to be a thief or an animal.
  b) He pretends to be his father.

4.11

Work in pairs. Answer these questions.

1 What does the poet have in his sandwiches? Do you think he has these every day? What sandwich would you have chosen?

2 What other things does the poet do because no one is around to stop him? Write down three things.

4.12

SKILLS
PAGE 30

Which thought below do you think is right? Write down the lines in the poem which make you think this.

1 The poet wishes he could be on his own more often as he has such fun.

2 The poet enjoys being on his own every now and then.

Writing interesting sentences

Remember that a sentence must make sense.

It must begin with a capital letter.——→ *A sentence must make sense.*

It should end with one of the following:

- full stop   .
- question mark   ?
- exclamation mark   !

4.14

Read Mike's diary entry. How does every sentence begin?

I was going to make a cake at school today. I had to get my
shopping done quickly as it was already 8.30am. I went in to
the supermarket and picked up a basket. I began my search.
I was lucky, the eggs and butter were in the first aisle.
I found the flour and fruit on the fifth aisle. I went to the
checkout. I paid £3.00 for my shopping. I stuffed all the
things in my bag. I ran all the way to school.

4.15

**Mike made his entry more interesting. He used different words to
start each sentence. Read it and make a list of the words he used.**

Today I was going to make a cake in school. Since it was
already 8.30am I had to get my shopping done quickly.
In the supermarket I picked up a basket. My search was
beginning. Luckily the eggs and butter were in the first
aisle. Flour and fruit were in the fifth aisle. At last I
could go to the checkout. Three pounds that lot cost
me! Quickly I stuffed all the things in my bag. Then I ran
all the way to school.

Read the next part of Mike's diary entry.

Match one of the words in the box below to each blank.
For example: For blank 1, choose the word 'The':

1 _____ first person I saw when I got to school
was Arty. 2 _____ course it would have been
a miracle if Arty had remembered to bring anything.
3 _____ soon as he saw my bag he looked
horrified. '4 _____ no, I've
forgotten my cake ingredients,' he yelled.
5 _____ were only ten minutes to go before the
bell went. 6 _____ if he ran all the way it would
take him seven minutes just to get to the shop.
7 _____ people have a way of looking at you.
'8 _____ worry, Arty,' I said. '9 _____
can share mine.' '10 _____ it's all right,' he said,
'I was only joking.'

Of	No	The	You	There
As	Oh	Even	Some	Don't

Think of a trick Mike could play back on Arty. Write at least five sentences saying what happened. Make sure each sentence begins with a different word.

4.18

SKILLS
PAGE 31

You are going to give a talk about what you enjoy doing in your spare time. Plan your talk.

Copy this diagram on to a new page. Write your hobby in the middle box.

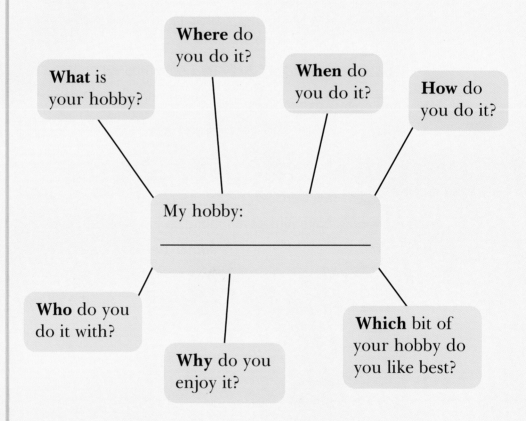

Where do
you do it?

What is
your hobby?

When do
you do it?

How do
you do it?

My hobby:
_____

Who do you
do it with?

Why do you
enjoy it?

Which bit of
your hobby do
you like best?

4.19

Decide what order you will answer the questions in when you give your talk. Number them in that order.

4.20

TRF
PAGE 27

**Make notes about how you will answer each question.
Write your notes in the order you have chosen.**

1 What is your hobby?

My hobby is …

4.21

TRF
PAGE 28

Work in pairs. Practise your talk.

Take it in turns to listen to each other.

If you are speaking:
- speak loudly and clearly
- make your sentences interesting
- don't be too 'chatty' as you will be speaking to a group and not just your friend.

If you are listening, **you must be ready to tell your friend:**
- if the talk is said slowly and loudly enough
- if there are any parts you do not understand
- anything that will make the talk better.

4.22

Now give your talk to the rest of the class.

UNIT 5

It's a challenge!

5.1 **Read the story opposite about a girls' football team.**

1 Stop when you reach a green box. What might happen next? Read on and see if you were right.

2 How do the girls in the story feel when they see Mrs Wilson?

3 What happens to Mrs Wilson during the game?

5.2 **Work in pairs. Note down words in the story which show that:**

1 Mrs Wilson is unfit.

2 Mrs Wilson does not know much about football.

3 Mrs Wilson played hockey a long time ago.

4 Mrs Wilson thinks the girls play well.

5 Mrs Wilson lands very heavily.

5.3

TRF
PAGE 30

SKILLS
PAGE 36

Write a description of Mrs Wilson. Look at the story to help you. Write at least one sentence about each of the questions below.

• What does Mrs Wilson look like?
• What does Mrs Wilson know about sport?
• What do you think of Mrs Wilson as a manager?

Hotshots!

There's a shock in store when we reach the pitch. There, standing in the centre circle, is our Geography teacher, Mrs Wilson. She has a football under her arm.

'I don't believe it,' says Tara. The other players gather
5 round, shocked.

Mrs Wilson is not the right shape for football. The purple tracksuit she's wearing does not make her look any thinner.

> **What is Mrs Wilson going to do?**

'Right, girls,' she says. 'I'm your new manager. What do you call yourselves? Hotshoots?'
10 'Hotshots,' says Lisa. 'Er, Mrs Wilson, do you know much about football?'

> **What do you think Mrs Wilson will say?**

'I'll have you know I was captain of the hockey team.' Mrs Wilson smiles at the memory. 'It's the same sort of
15 thing. Now who's going to bully off?'

'Bully off?' mutters Tara. 'What *is* she talking about?'

At first we play our normal game. We ignore Mrs Wilson as she huffs and puffs her way around the pitch. She keeps shouting things such as, 'Nice ball, Lisa!' and, 'Excellent shot!'
20 In fact, the game is going really well. Then Tara draws back her left foot and –

> **What do you think is going to happen?**

'Mrs Wilson!' I yell. Her back is turned. She is trying to shoo some boys away from the fence. 'Watch out!' Too late.

The ball lands like a cannonball against Mrs Wilson's back.
25 Oooooooof! Like a great **Californian redwood**, she keels over. I swear there is a faint earthquake as she hits the ground.

Adapted from *Pride and Penalties* by Terence Blacker

Californian redwood – a tree, famous for its enormous size

Stuck!

WOULD you have thought that a horse could get stuck on a jump during a race? That's just what happened at Sandown Race Course on Sunday.

There were only three horses in the race. Desert Challenger was struggling in third place. Then he stopped. Then he tried to climb over the last fence.

One keen race-goer said he had never seen anything like it. He said: 'He came running up to the fence flat out. Then he stopped. It was really strange. He lifted both legs at once and did not even try to jump it.'

The jockey, called **Sean** Fox, **dismounted**. Then the horse's trainer and some ground staff came to help.

After about ten minutes Desert Challenger was freed. Sean Fox **remounted**. But the horse was **disqualified** from the race. It had not carried its rider over all the fences.

A spokesperson for Sandown Race Course said that the incident looked bad for racing. 'However,' she said, 'this does not happen very often. When it does, you know the horse is very tired.'

She did not know when (or if) the horse would race again.

Adapted from *The Surrey Comet*,
14 November 1997

Sean – say his name: Shawn
dismounted – got off

remounted – got back on
disqualified – ruled out of the race

5.5

Work in pairs. What answers might Sean Fox give to the questions below?

1 How well was Desert Challenger running before he reached that fence?

Your answer might start: Desert Challenger was struggling …

2 How did Desert Challenger get stuck on the fence?

3 How long did it take to set Desert Challenger free?

4 What happened about the horse after the race?

5 What was wrong with Desert Challenger?

5.6

What order would these pictures be shown in on television?

5.7

TRF
PAGE 31

Work in pairs. You have your own radio show.

Tell your listeners what happened to Desert Challenger. Remember they cannot see what is happening. Use the pictures above to help you.

1 Write at least four short sentences. Each one should tell your listeners a main thing that happened.

2 Think about how you will say each sentence:

- When will you speak fast?
- When will you sound excited?
- When will you speak slowly?
- When will you sound worried?

3 Get together with another pair. Try out your radio reports on each other. You may like to make a tape recording.

5.8 The story on the opposite page is from a Greek myth. Read the 'Who's Who?' below to find out who is in it.

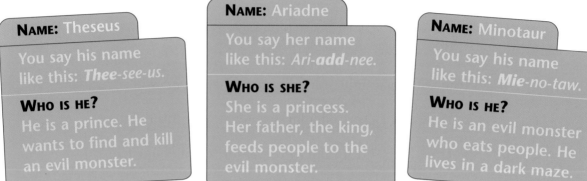

NAME: Theseus

You say his name like this: **Thee**-see-us.

WHO IS HE?
He is a prince. He wants to find and kill an evil monster.

NAME: Ariadne

You say her name like this: Ari-**add**-nee.

WHO IS SHE?
She is a princess. Her father, the king, feeds people to the evil monster.

NAME: Minotaur

You say his name like this: **Mie**-no-taw.

WHO IS HE?
He is an evil monster who eats people. He lives in a dark maze.

5.9 Now read the story. Theseus is entering the maze to find the monster.

5.10 Work on your own. Put these sentences in the right order so they tell the story you have just read.

1 The monster and Theseus fight very hard.

2 Theseus goes into the maze to look for the Minotaur.

3 Ariadne gives Theseus a ball of string.

4 Theseus kills the Minotaur.

5 The Minotaur bellows in Theseus' ear.

5.11

SKILLS
PAGE 37

Work in a group. Discuss your answers to these questions.

1 The story of Theseus and the Minotaur has been told for thousands of years. Some people think the story must be true. What do you think?

2 Can you name any other stories which have been told for thousands of years? Think of any fairy stories or religious stories that you know. Make a list.

3 Why do you think people still tell these stories today? Write down three of your reasons.

Theseus and the Minotaur

Theseus went down into the darkness. Then
he paused. He did not know which way to go.
   'Prince Theseus!'
   It was Ariadne. 'Here. Take this.' She
5 dropped down to him a ball of string. 'Even
if you kill the Minotaur, you won't find your way
back unless you use this.'
   'Great!' said Theseus. 'I could marry a girl like you!'
Then he tied one end of the string to the entrance and set
10 off. He unwound the string as he went.
   Theseus felt his way along the dark tunnel. It was true,
without the string he would have been hopelessly lost. He
was in a maze of winding corridors. Suddenly his fingers
brushed warm, wiry hair. Then he felt the bony curve of a
15 horn. The Minotaur bellowed in his ear. It flung him
through the darkness. It stamped on
him with sharp hooves. The string was knocked
out of his hand.
   They fought on in the darkness. The monster, who was
20 half-man and half-bull, crushed Theseus between hairy
arms. It lashed him with its tail. But Theseus took hold
of its horns. He twisted them first one way and then the
other. He kicked the beast, who butted and struggled. At
last the beast gave a gurgling gasp and fell dead.

Adapted from *Greek Myths* by Geraldine McCaughrean

Verbs

A **verb** is often an action word.

Fight, **flung** and **punched** are all verbs. They tell what someone or something is **doing**:

> The monster **punched** him.

5.13

Which verbs are shown in these pictures?

Work in a group. One of you thinks of a verb and acts it out. You must not speak. The others must guess what the verb is. The first person to guess is the next person to act.

5.15 Which two words in the list below are not verbs?

shouts   cave   eats   crushed   kicked   monster   dropped

5.16 Read the sentences below. Write down the verb in each one.

1 The monster bellowed loudly.

2 It flung him upwards.

3 They fought each other.

4 He killed the monster.

5.17

SKILLS
PAGES 38–39

Write about what happens in each of the pictures below.
Underline the verbs in your sentences.

You might start:
1 A knight <u>went</u> on a dangerous journey.
He <u>waved</u> goodbye and …

5.18

Read about Sir Gareth. He has to find the treasure hidden in the Caves of Mull. Then he must take it back to his castle.

Sir Gareth has a magic sword. He can turn his sword into anything he needs such as a ladder or a lamp…

He has a large, strong bag to carry the treasure in.

5.19

Work in pairs. Choose Sir Gareth's route through the Caves of Mull, opposite.

5.20

Talk about your chosen journey for Sir Gareth.

1 Describe each cave he visits.

2 What problem does he face in each cave?

3 How does he use his magic sword to overcome it?

4 How does he travel on? Use the verbs printed in yellow to help you.

5.21

Now get together with another pair. Tell your stories to each other.

5.22

Write about Sir Gareth's adventures in two of the caves. Use the words on the plan to help you. Make sure you write in sentences.

TRF
PAGE 34

> Sir Gareth rushed into the Fire Cave. The walls were on fire and the air was smoky …

The Caves of Mull

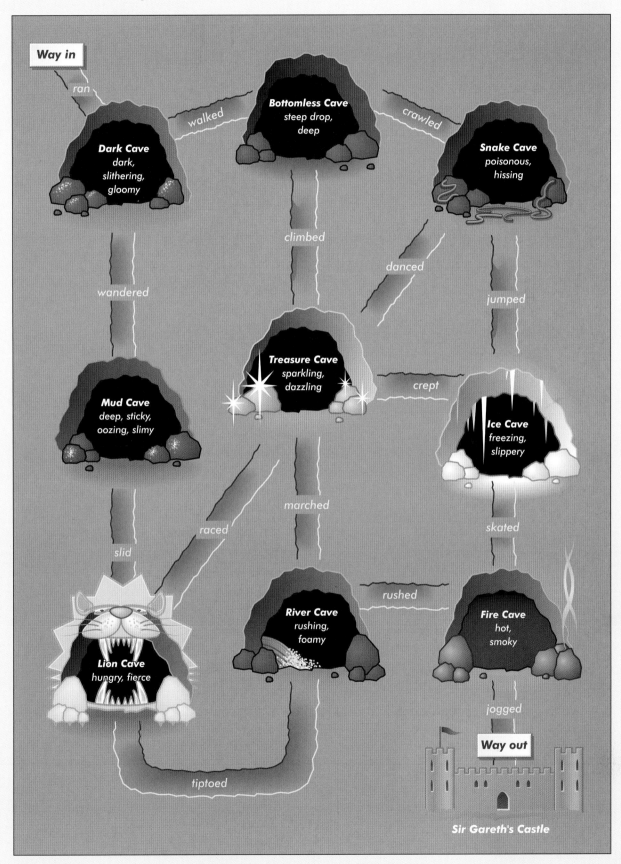

Way in

ran

Dark Cave
dark,
slithering,
gloomy

walked

Bottomless Cave
steep drop,
deep

crawled

Snake Cave
poisonous,
hissing

wandered

climbed

danced

jumped

Mud Cave
deep, sticky,
oozing, slimy

Treasure Cave
sparkling,
dazzling

crept

Ice Cave
freezing,
slippery

raced

marched

skated

slid

Lion Cave
hungry, fierce

rushed

River Cave
rushing,
foamy

Fire Cave
hot,
smoky

tiptoed

jogged

Way out

Sir Gareth's Castle

UNIT 6

Out and about

6.1

Read the story below. A class has gone on a trip to a wildlife park. Mr Angelo has a surprise for them …

Mr Angelo came out of the hut. An enormous American bald eagle was sitting on his arm. The assistant held a plastic bag and a thick black leather glove. Mr Angelo looked around. Then he pointed at Robert Warner.

5 'You, my boy, have the chance to give this splendid eagle its lunch. You can wear the glove and hold a piece of juicy, raw meat. The eagle will fly across and take the food from you!'

'Is he out of his mind?' Robert's eyes were popping open.

'Bye-bye, Robert,' someone called.

10 The assistant headed towards Robert. He was carrying the plastic bag full of oozing strips of beef in one hand. The black leather glove was in the other. Robert backed away.

'I'll do it.' Jennifer shot her hand up. 'Can I do it? It's so thrilling to even think of feeding a live eagle!'

15 Mr Angelo nodded. Jennifer got up. The assistant put the huge black leather glove on her right hand. He took a piece of dripping meat out of the plastic bag. He placed it on Jennifer's glove. Then he helped her hold her arm out straight.

20 'Don't be frightened,' he said. 'The eagle will only go for the meat. He will not go for your arm.'

'Ready?' Mr Angelo asked. 'Silence please.'

Mr Angelo released the eagle. It swept off his shoulder and into the air. The class cried out 'Ohhh!' as the bird's wings

25 spread out. It turned, swooping low over their heads. Some kids ducked. Jennifer stood straight and tall.

Then the eagle's claws reached down and grabbed the meat from Jennifer's glove. It flew back to Mr Angelo's shoulder and started chomping away on its snack.

30 Everyone cheered.

Adapted from City Safari *by Paul Zindell*

6.2

Put the pictures of the eagle having its lunch in the right order.
Write a sentence about what is happening in each one.

1 Picture b: Mr Angelo asked Robert to feed the eagle.
2 Picture …

6.3

Now find the answers to these questions.

1 Which three words say what kind of eagle Mr Angelo held?

2 Which three words describe the glove?

3 Find two words which make the meat sound juicy.

4 How did the eagle fly and take the meat?

When Mr Angelo released
   the eagle it …

Its wings …
The eagle turned …
Its claws …

6.4

SKILLS
PAGE 42

Write about your pet or an animal you have seen.

Use words which will help your reader picture what it is like.

1 My animal is …   2 When it feeds it …

3 When it sleeps it …   4 If you touch it, it feels …

6.5 Read the leaflet opposite. Then answer these questions.

    1 What would you do at Thunder River?

    2 Name two ways you can travel to Great Thorpe Farm.

    3 Where can you ride on an inflatable raft?

    4 Name two things which make the new ride *No Way Out* so scary.

    5 What height must you be over to go on *No Way Out*?

6.6 Work in pairs. Choose the two activities you would enjoy most.

    1 Which words in the leaflet make your activities sound fun?

    2 Why did you choose these activities? Make a list of reasons.

6.7 Imagine you have gone to Great Thorpe Park for the day. Write a postcard about your visit.

TRF
PAGE 36

SKILLS
PAGE 43

Name of person you are writing to

Dear Jane,
It's brilliant at Thorpe Park!
I went on a new ride called <u>No Way Out</u>. It was really scary.
We went backwards and it was pitch black. Then I saw a new born lamb at Thorpe Farm. It's been such a great day I don't want to leave! See you soon,

Love,

Rani

Your name

Address

Miss J. Peters

Flat 25

Spring House

Wandsworth

London SW18 9JR

1st

IT'S A GREAT DAY OUT...

Come to Great Thorpe Park for a great day out. There's lots to see, and lots to do. There are thrills **galore**, incredible rides and so much more besides. It's a world of fun and make believe, where everything and everyone is larger than life. It's big, it's giant, it's **humongous**... It's the Great Thorpe Park.

THUNDER RIVER

Hang on to your hats for white water rafting at Thunder River!

THORPE FARM

Take the Canada Creek Railway or the Waterbus to the Great Thorpe Farm. Everything on the farm is just as it was in the 1930s.

Come and make friends with the animals. You can walk freely among the rare breeds of sheep, goats and cattle.

LOGGERS LEAP

Our world famous water ride. It's wild, wet and wonderful!

DEPTH CHARGE

Take a deep breath in Fantasy Reef. Then ride an **inflatable** raft down a 13 metre waterslide.

WORLD FAMOUS NEW RIDE

X:\ No Way Out

Now open ... It's a world first. It's called **No Way Out**!

You'll need to strap yourself in and hold on tight for a terrifying ride backwards through total darkness.

It's only at the Great Thorpe Park. Dare you enter?

Once you do, there's no way out!
(**Height restriction 1.4 metres**)

---

galore – there are lots of them
humongous – huge
inflatable – filled with air

height restriction 1.4 metres – if you are less than 1.4 metres tall you cannot go on the ride

6.8
SEE ALSO
PAGE 20

Remember that a *noun* is a word used to name people, places or things. Which of the words below are nouns?

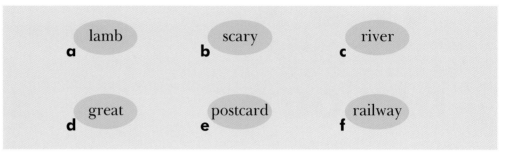

a lamb   b scary   c river

d great   e postcard   f railway

6.9
SEE ALSO
PAGE 30

Remember that a *proper noun* is the name given to a *particular* person or place. Which of the nouns below are proper nouns?

a Jane   b animal   c water

d Canada   e Newcastle   f park

6.10
SKILLS
PAGES 44–45

Work in pairs. Look at the map on the opposite page. Answer the questions below. Begin each proper noun with a capital letter.

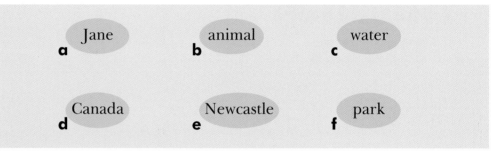

1 You are at Fen School. How do you get to the cinema?

2 You are at the cinema. How do you get to the chip shop?

3 You are at the chip shop. How do you get to Tan's house?

4 You are at Tan's house. How do you get to the sweet shop?

5 You are at the sweet shop. How do you get home?

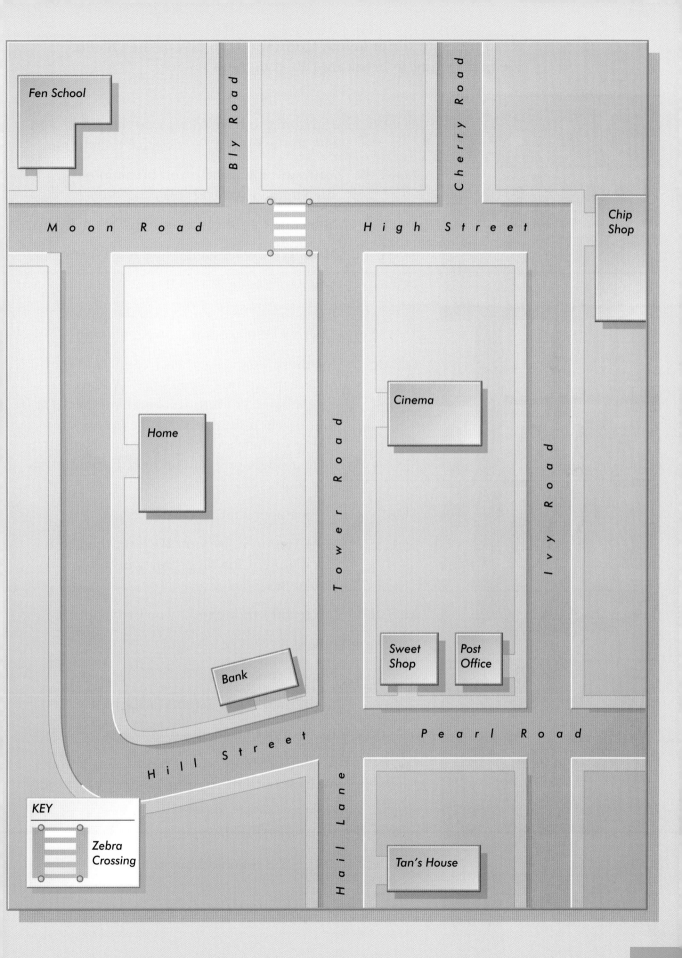

Fen School

Bly Road

Cherry Road

Chip Shop

Moon Road

High Street

Home

Tower Road

Cinema

Ivy Road

Bank

Sweet Shop

Post Office

Hill Street

Pearl Road

Hail Lane

KEY

Zebra Crossing

Tan's House

Read the play script below. Colin wants to talk to the Queen. He is planning to break into Buckingham Palace.

COLIN: I'm going to have to get into the palace and talk to the Queen. You'll have to help me.

ALISTAIR: You want me to help you break into Buckingham Palace?

COLIN: Someone has to come and give me a leg up.

ALISTAIR: Mum doesn't let me go into town by myself.

COLIN: You won't be by yourself, you'll be with me.

ALISTAIR: But you can't just climb into the palace. There'll be alarms and dogs and stuff.

COLIN: No there won't. Well, only corgis and they'll be asleep on the Queen's bed. A few years ago, a bloke got into Buckingham Palace at night. When the Queen woke up he was sitting on her bed, looking at her. He didn't have a single dog bite on him. He ended up in a loony bin.

ALISTAIR: I remember that … OK, I'll come.

COLIN: If he can do it, we can. We'll set the alarm clock tonight for three-thirty in the morning.

ALISTAIR: On second thoughts, I won't come.

COLIN: OK, stay! You're a wimp!

ALISTAIR: No, I'll come.

COLIN: Right then. Let's go and buy a rope.

ALISTAIR: But I'm not allowed out in traffic.

COLIN: Alistair, anybody would think a bus is going to drive onto the pavement especially to hit you.

ALISTAIR: Well, accidents happen, don't they?

COLIN: All right, I'll go and buy the rope myself.

ALISTAIR: I'll come.

Adapted from *Two Weeks with the Queen* by Mary Norris

6.12 | **Write down the answers to these questions.**

    1 Who does Colin want to talk to?

    2 How is Colin going to reach her?

    3 What two things does Alistair think might happen if Colin breaks into Buckingham Palace?

        He might set off the ...
        He might be attacked by ...

    4 What happened to the last person who broke into Buckingham Palace to meet the Queen?

6.13 | **Work in pairs. Answer the questions below. Use the words in the box to help you.**

worried	calm	thoughtful	carefree	brave	scared

    1 How would you describe Colin?

    2 How would you describe Alistair?

    Write down your answers like this:

    We think Colin is ...   because ...

    We think Alistair is ...   because ...

6.14 | **Write a story about what you think happens next. Use these questions to help you plan it.**

    1 Does Alistair choose to go with Colin?

    2 Does anyone try to stop the break-in?

    3 What might Colin want to talk to the Queen about?

    4 How do you think the story ends?

6.15

SKILLS

PAGE 46

You are going to learn how to write a short play. Look at how a script is laid out on the page.

speaker   *margin*   *speech*

ALISTAIR:	I remember that ... OK, I'll come.
COLIN:	If he can do it, we can. We'll set the alarm
	clock tonight for three-thirty in the morning.
ALISTAIR:	On second thoughts, I won't come.
COLIN:	OK, stay! You're a wimp!
ALISTAIR:	No, I'll come.
COLIN:	Right then. Let's go and buy a rope.

each speech starts on a new line   *each speech starts with a capital letter*

6.16

Now answer these questions in sentences. Your answers will give you a list of rules for writing a play script.

1 Where do you put the name of the person who is speaking?

You put the name of the person who is speaking in ...

2 What kind of letters do you use to write the speaker's name?

3 What does the piece of punctuation after the speaker's name look like?

4 Where does each speech start?

5 What does each speech start with?

6.17

Get ready to write your short play. Read what has happened so far. Decide what happens next.

> Mrs Thomas has taken her biology class to a wildlife park. The pupils are allowed to touch and play with some of the smaller animals. Sam really likes the tortoise. Gita likes the rat. It is nearly time to go home, but Sam and Gita do not want to leave the animals behind.

6.18

PAGE 37

Work in pairs. These are the people in your play. Write two sentences for each one. Say what you think each character is like.

Mrs Thomas (Mrs T)	the Biology teacher
Gita (*Gee-ta*)	a pupil
Sam	a pupil
Mr Davis (Mr D)	the wildlife park keeper

6.19

PAGES 38–39

Work in pairs. Follow the guide below. Decide what each person will say. Then write the play script.

GITA:	I really like this rat. I don't want to leave it here.
SAM:	_____ .
GITA:	_____ .
SAM:	_____ .
MRS T:	Come on, you two. It's time to get on the coach and go back to school.
GITA:	_____ .
SAM:	_____ .
MRS T:	_____ .
MR D:	_____ .
SAM:	_____ .

6.20

Now act out your play.

UNIT 7

It makes me mad!

7.1
SKILLS
PAGE 49

Read the story about Swapper on the opposite page. Answer the questions below.

1 Why do people call Stephen 'Swapper'?

2 Why does Swapper put all his gear at the end of the yard?

3 Why do you think no one touches anything until Swapper says so?

4 How does Swapper behave towards people?

5 What is Swapper's rule?

7.2

Work in pairs. One of you is Swapper, the other is Swapper's friend. Make up their conversation.

Swapper's friend:
- You have a poster of Swapper's favourite football team.
- You want to swap it for some stickers.
- What three things will you say about the poster to make Swapper agree to the swap?

Swapper:
- You want to get more than one poster for the stickers.
- What three things will you say to make your friend swap more things?

7.3

Get together with another pair. Take it in turns to act out the conversations you have made up. Which ideas worked best? Why?

7.4

Would you like Swapper to be your friend? Which parts of the story make you feel this way? Give reasons for your answer.

Swapper

Swapping's great – if it's for fun. But with
Stephen it was different. For him it was for real.
That's why no one called him Stephen. They
called him Swapper.

5   No one knew where he got all his gear. Or
what he did with it afterwards. At break time he'd
lay it all out under the shelter at the far end of
the yard. This was a long way from the staff room
window. It was like a car boot sale. There was
10 always a crowd there, looking. You didn't touch
until Swapper told you.

He wasn't tall. He wasn't broad. He was thin
and pale. In cold weather the end of his nose was
like a red button. His eyebrows and lashes were so
15 light they were invisible. But his eyes were dark
and looked right through you.

When you did a deal with Swapper you lost. As
you walked away you had this feeling – I've been
swindled. How it happened, you couldn't say.
20 Swapper would look at what you wanted. He
looked at what you had in your hand. Then his
nose wrinkled.

'You kidding? That's rubbish.'

'Where d'you get it? Out of a cornflake packet?'

25 'That's a swap? That's robbery.'

He went on until you started feeling in your
pocket for something else to add to what you
were offering. Even though you knew you were
crazy. Then it would vanish into his pocket.

30 You walked away looking at what Swapper gave
you and wondering why you wanted it in the first
place.

It was no good going back and saying, *I've
changed my mind*. No swap back was Swapper's
35 rule. Swapper was for real.

Adapted from *Swapper* by Robert Leeson

7.5 The Blue Cross is a charity. It tries to stop people being cruel to animals. Read its advertisement on the opposite page.

7.6 Each sentence below is untrue. Write a correct sentence instead. The first one has been done for you.

1 Tiny was found on a motorway.
Tiny was found in a rubbish bin.

2 Tiny was only three weeks old when he was found.

3 The staff fed Tiny every five hours.

4 The Blue Cross does not mind destroying healthy animals.

5 You have to give at least £10 to help an animal.

7.7

SKILLS
PAGE 50

Work in groups. The advertisement tries to make you give to The Blue Cross. Answer the questions below.

1 Look at the heading. Who will read the advertisement?

2 Describe what the kitten in the picture looks like. How does it make you feel?

3 Look at lines 1–3. List three words which make you feel sorry for the kitten.

4 Look at line 4. List three main things you found out about the kitten.

5 Look at lines 6–11. What three main things do you learn about The Blue Cross?

6 Does the advertisement make you want to:
a) find out how you can help?
b) send money?
Why?

Animal LOVERS?

Dumped in a rubbish bin and left to die ...
Just £2 a month could save him.

He was hungry and frightened, and calling for his mother.
Tiny was only four weeks old and barely alive when he was
5   brought to The Blue Cross ...

We never gave up. For weeks our caring staff looked after the little
kitten. To begin with he needed to be fed every two hours.

At last he was safe. The Blue Cross had kept its promise. We will
never put down a healthy animal just because it has no home.

10   We need real animal lovers like you to help us. Then we can
save the lives of other unwanted pets like Tiny.

Please fill in the coupon below to find out how you can help.

Please send me more information about how I can help animals
like Tiny. I would like to make a gift to The Blue Cross.

Name (Mr/Ms) _____

Address _____

_____

Postcode _____

Send to The Blue Cross, Freepost, Room 904C, Shilton Road, Burford, Oxon OX18 4BR.

7.8 **Read the poem on the opposite page. It is about how much the poet hates car stickers. Then answer the questions below.**

1 The poet has counted up the number of stickers the driver has in his window. How many does he say there are?

2 Four of the stickers tell you something about the driver of the car. Which are they? What do they tell you?

   1 The sticker says there is a dog on board.
      The driver must own a dog.

3 Look at line 3.
   a) Which magical person normally rides on a broomstick?
   b) What is the driver saying his wife is like?
   c) Do you think the wife would be pleased?

4 What else does the poem say the driver has in his car apart from stickers?

5 Look at the last two lines of the poem. What does the poet think about the driver of this car?

7.9 **Work in pairs. Write and design four stickers you would put on a car window. Make them as funny and interesting as you can.**

7.10 **What makes *you* mad? Why does it make you mad? Write three sentences about it. Start your piece of writing with one of these:**

1 I hate … because …

2 The worst thing you can do to me is … because …

3 I can't stand people who … because …

4 When I see … it makes me mad because …

Stickers

I can't bear all those car rear-windows
Plastered with daft words;
My **missus** *drives a broomstick* – that is
Strictly for the birds.

5   I don't care if he *loves his Mini*,
Has a *Dog on board*
Or if he is a *Spurs supporter*
Or where he's been abroad.

Keep your distance – he should worry!
10 Not at any price
Would **I** **venture** any closer
To his fluffy dice.

Short vehicle. Not long, **you geddit?**
What a **witty spread!**
15 A dozen stickers on his window,
Nothing in his head.

By Vernon Scannell

missus – his wife
venture – come
you geddit? – this is short for 'do you get it?'
witty spread – all the funny stickers

Adverbs

1 Remember that a verb is often an *action* word. It tells what someone or something is *doing*.

> Ben **drove** slowly along the road.

verb (action word)

2 An **adverb** usually tells *how* the action is being done.
Ask yourself: *how* did Ben drive along the road?

> Ben drove **slowly** along the road.

adverb (how the action is being done)

Slowly is an adverb. Adverbs often end with the letters **–ly**.

Work in groups of four.

Pair 1	Pair 2
Choose a verb and an adverb from the lists below. Act out your verb in the way described by your adverb. The other pair have to guess which verb and adverb you have chosen.	Watch the other pair act out their chosen verb and adverb. Say what they are doing. For example: walking quickly. If you are right, it is your turn to act.

Verbs	Adverbs
singing	happily
painting	quietly
walking	sleepily
eating	jerkily
jumping	quickly

7.13

Write out the sentences below. Fill in the gaps with adverbs which make Katie sound sad. Choose your adverbs from the box.

Katie opened her letter and sighed
_____ . She went _____ out
of the house. As she walked along she sang
_____ .When she arrived at Mike's
house she knocked on the door _____ .

sadly
loudly
quietly
happily
quickly
cheerily
slowly
moodily

7.14

Write out the above sentences again. This time choose adverbs from the box which make Katie sound happy.

7.15

TRF
PAGE 41

SKILLS
PAGE 51

Look at the cartoon below. Write five sentences about it. Use an adverb from the box below in each sentence. Underline it.

quickly   happily   worriedly
sadly   loudly   carefully   slowly
anxiously   stupidly   lovingly

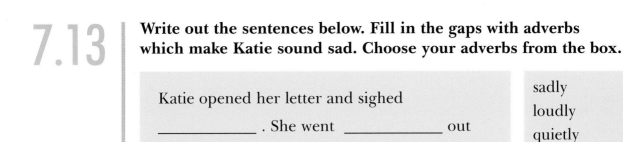

7.16 You and your friend went to hear your favourite band in concert last Saturday. Read the notes below to find out what happened. Find the adverb in each note.

1 The support group was late and played badly.

2 When your favourite band came on, the lead singer spoke rudely. He said the audience was 'boring' and 'lazy'.

3 The music was played so loudly that you couldn't hear the words. Your ears hurt for three days afterwards.

4 The ice-creams sold out quickly. Only soft drinks were left and they cost £2.50! They weren't even cold.

7.17 Write a letter to the people who organised the concert.

Tell them why you did not enjoy it. Ask for your money back. Be polite. Use the notes below to help you plan your letter.

1 My friend and I came to hear our favourite band in concert last …

2 First of all the support band …

3 Then when our favourite band came on, the lead singer …

4 The music was …

5 When we went for an ice-cream …

6 We felt very let down by the concert. We would like to ask for …

Check that all your sentences:
- make sense   - start with a capital letter   - end with a full stop.

7.18 Now write your letter. The notes on the opposite page show you how to write and lay out your letter.

TRF
PAGE 42

SKILLS
PAGES 52–53

23 Westfield Way

Tenton

Sussex

PO20 7YX

18 August 1998

Dear Mr Anderson

My friend and I came to hear our favourite band in concert _____ . We were looking forward to it very much.

First of all the support band _____ . Then when our favourite band came on, the lead singer _____ . The music was _____ . When we went for an ice-cream _____ .

We felt very let down by the concert. We would like to ask for _____ .

I look forward to hearing from you.

Yours sincerely

Clare M. Constant

CLARE M. CONSTANT

8.1 **Read the story opposite. It was written over 100 years ago.**
It is about a schoolgirl called Jane Eyre (you say Eyre like *air*). Jane
has been sent away to boarding school. Mr Brocklehurst has come to
check up on the school. Jane does not want him to see her.

8.2 **Put these pictures in the order of the story.**

A   B   C   D

8.3

TRF
PAGE 44

**Work in a group. List the differences between Jane's school and
your school.**

8.4

SKILLS
PAGES 56–57

Jane keeps a diary. Write her entry for the day.

I was in …

My slate …

I felt …

Mr Brocklehurst …

I had to …   I felt …

Jane Eyre

I had sat well back on the bench. I hoped he would not see me. While I was busy with my sum I held the slate up so it hid my face.

My slate somehow slipped from my hand. CRASH!
5 Every eye was upon me. I knew it was all over now.

'A careless girl!' said Mr Brocklehurst. 'It is the new pupil. I must not forget I have something to say about her.'

Then loudly (how very loud it seemed to me!) he said,
10 'Let the child who broke her slate come forward.'

Two girls sitting on either side of me set me on my feet. They pushed me towards him.

'Fetch that stool,' said Mr Brocklehurst. He pointed to a very high one. It was brought to him.

15 'Place the child upon it.'

And I was placed there. I don't know who by. I only know I was pushed up on to the stool. And then I was level with Mr Brocklehurst's nose. He was standing a yard away from me.

20 'Ladies,' said he, turning to his own family. Then, 'Teachers, and children, do you see this girl?'

Of course they did. I felt their eyes burning into my skin.

'You see she is still young? Yet who would think she is
25 already wicked? My dear children, you must be on your guard against her. Teachers, you must watch her. You must know that this girl is a liar!'

'How shocking,' said Mr Brocklehurst's wife.

'Let her stand half an hour longer on the stool.
30 Let no one speak to her for the rest of the day,' Mr Brocklehurst ordered.

And there I was left. I had to stand on the stool until the schoolroom was dark. No one spoke to me.

Adapted from Jane Eyre *by Charlotte Brontë*

slate – pupils used to write on black slates with chalk

8.5

Read Zlata's diary entry on the opposite page.

Zlata lives in Sarajevo (you say it like this: *Sa – ra – yeah – vo*). She should be at school but there is a war going on.

8.6

Answer these questions.

1 Read lines 3–4. Which five words show how Zlata feels?

2 Read lines 5–11. What does Zlata miss about school?

3 Which foods does Zlata have to do without?

4 Read lines 12–16. What is happening in the war?

5 Read lines 17 to the end. Why does Zlata feel so sad?

8.7

TRF
PAGE 45

SKILLS
PAGE 58

A film is going to be made about how Zlata's life has changed.

Make a storyboard of four pictures for the film. Each one should show how Zlata's life has changed. Look at the diary extract to help you. Write the words Zlata will say with each picture. The first shot has been done for you.

1

I used to be able to go to school. Now...

Zlata's Diary

Monday, 29th June 1992

Dear **Mimmy**,

BOREDOM!!! SHOOTING!!! SHELLING!!! PEOPLE BEING
KILLED!!! DESPAIR!!! HUNGER!!! MISERY!!! FEAR!!!

5 That's my life! The life of an innocent eleven-year-old
schoolgirl!!! A schoolgirl without a school, without the
fun and excitement of school. A child without games,
without friends, without the sun, without birds,
without nature, without fruit, without chocolate or
10 sweets, with just a little powdered milk. In short, a
child without a childhood. A wartime child.

I now realise that I am really living through a war.
I am witnessing an ugly, disgusting war. I and
thousands of other children are suffering. We are
15 seeing this town being destroyed. We are crying,
weeping and seeking help. But we do not get any.

God, will this ever stop? Will I ever be a schoolgirl
again? Will I ever enjoy my childhood again?

I once heard that childhood is the most wonderful
20 time of your life. And it is. I loved it. And now an
ugly war is taking it all away from me. Why?

I feel sad. I feel like crying.
I am crying.

Your Zlata

Adapted from *Zlata's Diary* by Zlata

Mimmy – Zlata calls her diary
by this name

8.8   **Read the poem on the opposite page. Then answer the questions.**

8.9   **Look at stanzas (verses) 1–3. How does the poet describe the caretaker?**

    1   The caretaker was a …

    2   The caretaker's nose was …

    3   The caretaker was scary because he …
       (Find three reasons.)

    4   The caretaker wore …

8.10   **Work in pairs. Look at stanzas 4–6. The poet has now grown up. Answer these questions.**

    1   Look at stanza 4. Which words make you feel sorry for the caretaker?

    2   Look at stanza 5. What does the poet think about grown-ups now that he has grown up himself?

    3   Look at the last stanza, then look back at the first stanza. Why do you think that the poet has changed the third line in the last stanza?

8.11

TRF
PAGE 46

What do you think about the poem? Write at least one sentence about each of the points below.

   •   What did the caretaker seem like when the poet was a boy?
   •   What does the caretaker seem like when the poet is grown up?
   •   Why have the poet's feelings about the caretaker changed?
   •   What do you like or dislike about the poem?

The School Caretaker

1   In the corner of the playground
    Down dark and slimy stairs,
    Lived a Monster with a big nose
    Full of curly hairs.

2   He had a bunch of keyrings
    Carved out of little boys,
    He **confiscated** comics
    And all our favourite toys.

3   He wore a greasy uniform,
    Looked like an undertaker,
    More scary than a horror film,
    He was the school caretaker.

4   I left the school some years ago;
    Saw him again the other day.
    He looked rather sad and old
    Shuffling on his way.

5   It's funny when you grow up
    How grown-ups start growing down,
    And the **snarls** upon their faces
    Are no more than a frown.

6   In the corner of the playground
    Down dark and slimy stairs.
    Sits a lonely little man
    With a nose full of curly hairs.

By Brian Patten

confiscated – the pupils were
    not allowed to have toys or
    comics in school, so the
    caretaker took them away
snarls – frightening, bad-
    tempered looks

8.12

You are going to learn how to join two sentences together.

Look at the two sentences below:

A *The caretaker was scary. He looked like a monster.*

They could be joined together to make one long sentence:

B *The caretaker was scary because he looked like a monster.*

8.13

Can you see the differences between A and B? Check against the notes below.

full stop has been removed   *'because' has been added*

*The caretaker was scary **because** he looked like a monster.*

no capital letter is needed

8.14

To join sentences together you need the right joining word. Joining words are called *connectives* because they *connect* sentences.

These connectives are often used:

when	and	but	because	or	so	if	as

8.15

Each sentence below has a missing connective. Write out each sentence. Fill in the missing connective from the box above.

1 The caretaker found some fireworks _____ the party was over.

2 He discovered who they belonged to _____ he did not return them.

3 He said you had to be careful with fireworks _____ an accident could happen.

4 The school put on a special firework display _____ lots of people went.

8.16

Join the pairs of sentences below to make one sentence. Write each new sentence you make. Use a different connective from the box each time.

so	but	because	and	if	as

1 The youth club didn't have a driver for their visit to the fire station.
  They asked my dad to help out.

2 We only just got there in time.
  We were running late.

3 A fireman showed us how to put out a small fire.
  We took it in turns to help him.

4 We enjoyed setting off the sirens.
  We thought the noise was too loud.

5 We had a chance to see the fire team in action.
  When we were leaving the alarm went off.

Check that you have taken away one full stop and one capital letter when you joined the sentences together.

8.17

TRF
PAGE 47

SKILLS
PAGE 59

Now you are going to write some long sentences of your own. They have already been started for you.

1 The fireman raced up the ladder **but** …

2 He had difficulty breaking in **because** …

3 Two friends were gasping for breath **and** …

4 They thought they could not last **until** …

5 The fireman said it could have been too late **if** …

What do you remember most about this school year?

Choose four of the headings below. Use them to help you write about your memories. Begin each memory on a new line. Write at least one long sentence for each memory. Use some of the joining words below.

and	but	because	yet	so	if	as	until

1 The best day was …
It might be the day when:
- you went on a trip somewhere
- someone interesting came
- you did something special.
Write about what happened.
Say why you enjoyed it so much.

2 What I think about the lessons I've been to.
  a) My best subject was …
     Say why you like it so much.
  b) My worst subject was …
     Say why you dislike it so much.

3 My most embarrassing moment was …
What happened?
Why did it make you feel embarrassed?

4 The hardest thing I had to do this year was ...
What was it?
Why was it so hard?

5 My friends are ...
They have been great
because ...
Describe your closest friends.
Why are you such good
friends with each of them?
What fun things have
you done together?

**6 When my teachers
talked about me in the
staffroom, they said ...**
You'll just have to make
this one up!

TRF
PAGE 51

SKILLS
PAGES 4,
11, 16, 47

Know your letters

The alphabet can be written in small case letters or capital letters.
This is the alphabet in small case letters:

a b c d e f g h i j k l m n o p q r s t u v w x y z

This is the alphabet in capital letters:

A B C D E F G H I J K L M N O P Q R S T U V W X Y Z

9.1 **Work in pairs. One of you says a letter in the alphabet. Say whether it is a capital or small case letter. Your friend writes it down.**

> *You say 'capital F' – your friend would write down F.*

> *You say 'small case f' – your friend would write down f.*

9.2 **Work on your own. Look at the order of the letters in the alphabet. Answer these questions.**

1 Which letter comes after k?

2 Which letter comes before g?

3 Which letter is three letters after w?

4 Which letter is two letters before d?

5 Write these letters out in alphabetical order:

t r n b i q v z a

There are two sorts of letters in the alphabet.
They are called **vowels** and **consonants.**

Vowels

The following letters are vowels:

a e i o u

Sometimes **y** can act as a vowel (as in the word **dry**).
Every word must have at least one vowel in it.

9.3

Write out the vowels in these words:

1 bake   **2** radio   **3** music   **4** travel   **5** shopping

9.4

How many vowels are there in each of these words?

1 hello   **2** tree   **3** concert   **4** sunshine   **5** chocolate

Consonants

All the other letters in the alphabet are called consonants:
b c d f g h j k l m n p q r s t v w x y z
Sometimes **y** can act as a consonant (as in the word **yellow**).

9.5

Write out the consonants in these words:

1 name   **2** junk   **3** shout   **4** gloves   **5** computer

9.6

How many consonants are there in each of these words?

1 bud   **2** start   **3** carrot   **4** pocket   **5** hamster

Capital letters

You must begin a sentence with a capital letter:

It had started snowing late in the evening.

9.7

Write out the sentences below. Put in the missing capital letters.

when he woke up it was really cold. it was as if the world was covered in white foam. even the cars had disappeared.

SEE ALSO
PAGE 30

You must use a capital letter to begin a proper noun.

A proper noun is the name given to a particular place or person:

person: *Ben, Gita*
place: *Birmingham*

Capital letters should also be used for:

days of the week:	*Monday, Tuesday*
months of the year:	*January, February*
names of specific events:	*World Cup, Christmas*
brand names:	*Nike, Pepsi*

9.8

Write out the sentences below. Add the missing capital letters.

1 It was the thursday before christmas when the car broke down.

2 Dad said the old ford fiesta had been playing up since they went to london in it.

3 They had gone in may to see the final of the FA cup at wembley.

Full stops

A full stop looks like this .

A full stop often ends a sentence.

Ben put his Walkman on and listened to the radio.

9.9

Read the advertisement below. Write it out. Put in the missing full stops.

Please help us raise money for the Night Shelter We are holding a New Year's Eve disco It is on Wednesday 31st December at Roath Park The tickets are £4 each

You can ring 646589 for details

Check that you have put in five full stops.

9.10

Write out the sentences below. Put in the missing full stops and capital letters.

Ben went home and dialled the number he got all the details about the disco later on he rang Gita, Andy and Kate they all agreed to go to the disco together it would be great fun and help raise money for the Night Shelter

Check that you have put in five full stops and four capital letters.

Exclamation marks

SKILLS
PAGE 26

An exclamation mark looks like this **!**

Some sentences end with an exclamation mark instead of a full stop. Use an exclamation mark when you want to show that someone is:

Angry:	How dare you!
Excited:	That concert was brilliant!
Scared:	Let's get out of here!

9.11

Three of these sentences should end with an exclamation mark. Write them out correctly.

1 It was Kate's birthday.

2 She had been given a lovely new sweatshirt.

3 It looked fantastic.

4 Kate's day at school seemed to go on for ever and ever.

5 She couldn't wait to race back home.

9.12

Write out the sentences below. Add five full stops and two exclamation marks.

Kate walked into the house It was in darkness She opened the lounge door What a surprise All her friends were there They had a cake covered in candles They all started singing Happy Birthday to You

Question marks

SKILLS
PAGE 15

A question mark looks like this **?**

Questions start with a capital letter and end with a question mark:

Where are you going?

9.13

Which of these sentences should end with a question mark? Write them out correctly.

1 I bumped into Kate

2 What are you doing on Saturday

3 I'm going to see a film

4 When did you decide to go

5 Why don't you join me

9.14

SKILLS
PAGE 46

Match up the parts of the sentences below. Write them down. Add a question mark *or* an exclamation mark to the end of each one.

1 Where are   **a** with you

2 It's a   **b** be lovely

3 Can I come   **c** you going

4 Yes, that would   **d** big surprise

Speech marks

When someone speaks in a cartoon, what they say is put inside a speech bubble:

Have you seen Jenny?

She went that way!

In writing, speech marks are used instead of speech bubbles:

open speech marks "Have you seen Jenny?" *close speech marks*

"She went that way!"

9.15

Write out the speeches below. Put in the missing speech marks.

1 Do you want to go to a party tonight?

2 I am already going to one.

3 Where is that?

4 It's at Mark's house.

5 That's where I am going too.

9.16

Write out the words you think the people in the cartoon are saying. Put them in speech marks instead of in bubbles.

Look at the speech below:

The speech marks are only around the words that Jenny actually says.

"That was the worst party I have ever been to," said Jenny.

*Punctuation is **inside** the speech marks.*

9.17

SKILLS

PAGE 33

Write out the sentences below. Put speech marks around the words the person is actually saying.
Copy all the other words and punctuation carefully.

1 That was the worst party I have ever been to, said Jenny.

2 Why was it so bad? asked Robert.

3 There were so many people there, said Jenny.

4 What is wrong with that? asked Robert.

5 They were all over sixty, said Jenny.

Spelling

Follow these five steps. They will help you learn to spell any word.

Step 1: LOOK / LEARN **Look** carefully at the word and learn it.	*h o l i d a y*
Step 2: SAY **Spell** the word out loud several times.	*h-o-l-i-d-a-y*
Step 3: COVER **Cover** up the word so you cannot see it.	
Step 4: WRITE **Write** the word out.	*holiday*
Step 5: CHECK **Check** how the word is spelled.	*holiday* *holiday*

Use these steps to learn the spellings for: friend, beautiful, Wednesday.

REMEMBER!

When you want to learn a spelling:

Look ⟶ Say ⟶ Cover ⟶ Write ⟶ Check

Spelling words which are two words joined together

Look at the word you want to learn to spell. Is it made by joining two words together? If so, you can remember and spell the word in two parts.

For example:

news + paper

rail + way

table + cloth

foot + stool

9.18 **Two words were joined together to make each of the words below. Write out the two words.**

1 bookcase
   book case

2 earthquake

3 bedroom

4 nowhere

5 lighthouse

9.19 **Look at the two lists below. Take one word from list A and join it to a word in list B to make a new word. Write down your new word.**

A	B
week	work
day	bite
patch	end
body	light
frost	guard

TRF
PAGES 60–61
PAGES 74, 79

SKILLS
PAGES 54–55
PAGE 27

Spelling words which can be broken into parts

Look at the word you want to learn to spell. Can it be broken into smaller parts? If so, you can remember and spell the word in smaller parts.

For example:

untouched can be broken into three parts:

un	touch	ed
prefix	*stem*	*suffix*

The main part of the word is called the **stem**.
The part added to the front of the word is called the **prefix**.
The part added to the end of the word is called the **suffix**.

9.20

Join each word below with a prefix from the box to make another word.

| dis | un | mis | after |

1 kind
unkind

2 noon

3 take

4 able

9.21

Join each word below with a suffix from the box to make another word.

1 power
powerful

2 base

3 think

4 fix

| ful | ment | ed | ing |

9.22

The words below have a prefix and a suffix. Write each word out as three parts.

	prefix	root	suffix
Unreasonable			
disappointed			

Spelling words which have letter patterns

Look at the word you want to learn to spell. Does it have a group of letters in it which can be found in many other words? Find these groups of letters and remember how to spell them. It will help you spell the whole word.

For example:
All the words below have **atch** in them:
w**atch**   m**atch**   c**atch**   h**atch**   l**atch**

9.23

How many words can you write which start with st?

stop, start, star ...

9.24

Sort the pictures below into three groups.

1   Write down the last two letters of each word.
2   Then write out the words which belong to each of these groups.

an group	**at** group	**en** group
can	hat	pen
...	...	...

Heinemann is an imprint of Pearson Education Limited,
a company incorporated in England and Wales, having
its registered office at Edinburgh Gate, Harlow, Essex, CM20 2JE.
Registered company number:872828

First published 1998

10 09
10

ISBN 978 0 435105 41 9
Designed and typeset by Gecko Ltd
Illustrated by Phil Healey, Steve Lach, Pantelis Palios, Chris Ryley,
Jamie Sneddon, Gary Wing and Gecko Ltd
Cover design by MCC
Printed and bound in China (CTPS/10)

Acknowledgements

The Authors and Publishers dedicate this book to the memory of Kay Wills. Clare Constant thanks Matthew for all
his support and patience during the writing of this book.

The Authors and Publishers would like to thank the following for permission to use copyright material.

Penguin Books Ltd for extracts adapted from *Video Rose* by Jacqueline Wilson (Blackie's Children's Books) p5,
Zlata's Diary by Zlata Filipovic p77 and for the poem 'The School Caretaker' from *Gargling with Jelly* by Brian
Patten; *Jimmy Jet and his TV Set* from *Where The Sidewalk Ends* by Shel Silverstein © 1974 by Evil Eye Music, inc. by
permission of Edite Kroll Literary Agency Inc, p8; Jennifer Luithlen Agency on behalf of Robert Swindells for an
adapted extract from 'What's for Dinner?' in *No More School*, Methuen, p15; Cadbury Ltd for the Caramel wrapper
p16; Viking Children's Books for 'Shoplifting' by Mick Gower from *Criminal Records* p18; Colin West for adapted
extracts from 'Small Ads' in *Never Say Boo to a Ghost and Other Haunting Rhymes*, Ed. Foster and Paul, Oxford
University Press, p24; David Higham Associates on behalf of Penelope Lively for an adapted extract from 'A
Martian Comes to Stay' in *Uninvited Ghosts*, Mammoth, p27; Random House (UK) Ltd for the adapted extract from
The Daydreamer by Ian McEwan published by Jonathan Cape Ltd 1994 p35; Trevor Millum for his poem 'Alone in
the House' from *Warning: Too much Schooling Can Damage Your Health* by Trevor Millum, Thomas Nelson & Sons
Ltd, p38; Macmillan Children's Books for an adapted extract from *Pride and Penalties* by Terence Blacker p45, and
from *Two Weeks with the Queen* by Morris Gleitzman p60; The Surrey Comet and Guardian Newspaper for an
adapted extract from the article 'I'm knackered' by Marcus Priaulx, 14 November 1997, p46; Orchard Books Ltd
for an adapted extract from *Greek Myths* by Geraldine McCaughrean first published in Great Britain by Orchard
Books, a division of the Watts Publishing Group, 96 Leonard Street, London EC2A 4RH, p48; Curtis Brown Ltd,
New York, on behalf of Paul Zindell for an adapted extract from *City Safari* copyright 1993 by Paul Zindel, first
published in the USA by Bantam Doubleday Dell entitled *Fifth Grade Safari*, p54; Thorpe Park for adapted extracts
from their leaflet 'Great Thorpe Park' p57; Reed Consumer Books Ltd for an extract from *Swapper* by Robert
Leeson, Mammoth, p65; The Blue Cross for an advertisement p66; Random House UK Ltd for the poem 'Stickers'
by Vernon Scannell from *Travelling Light*, Bodley Head, p68.

The Publishers have made every effort to trace the copyright holders, but if they have inadvertently overlooked
any, they will be pleased to make the necessary arrangements at the first opportunity.

The Publishers would like to thank the following for permission to reproduce photographs on the pages noted.

The British Museum, p28; The Surrey Comet, p46; RSPCA p67; Penguin Books, p77.